ASA-SE-1

THE STANDARD® ENGINE LOG
SE-1

ASA-SE-1
ISBN 978-1-56027-416-2

Published by
Aviation Supplies & Academics, Inc.
7005 132nd Place SE
Newcastle, Washington 98059 USA
Website: asa2fly.com
Email: asa@asa2fly.com

Printed in the United States of America

[19] 23

TRANSPORTATION USD $8.95

Engine Record General Information

Manufacturer ______________________ **Model** ______________________

Serial ______________________ **Type Certificate** ______________________

This engine is currently installed in aircraft: ______________________

____

Minimum Octane Fuel ______________ **Oil Grade:** Summer ______________ Winter ______________

Magneto Time ______________ **Point Setting** ______________ **Firing Order** ______________

Spark Plug Gap ______________

Manufacturer's Recommended Overhaul at ______________ **hours**

Registered Owner Record

Name ______________________ Address ______________________

City ______________ State ________ From ______________ To ______________

Name ______________________ Address ______________________

City ______________ State ________ From ______________ To ______________

Name ______________________ Address ______________________

City ______________ State ________ From ______________ To ______________

Name ______________________ Address ______________________

City ______________ State ________ From ______________ To ______________

Name ______________________ Address ______________________

City ______________ State ________ From ______________ To ______________

Name ______________________ Address ______________________

City ______________ State ________ From ______________ To ______________

Notes

YEAR 20____ DATE	RECORDING TACH TIME	TODAY'S FLIGHT	TOTAL TIME IN SERVICE	**Description of Inspections, Tests, Repairs and Alterations** Entries must be endorsed with Name, Rating and Certificate Number of Technician or Repair Facility. (See back pages for other specific entries.)

YEAR 20____ DATE	RECORDING TACH TIME	TODAY'S FLIGHT	TOTAL TIME IN SERVICE	**Description of Inspections, Tests, Repairs and Alterations** Entries must be endorsed with Name, Rating and Certificate Number of Technician or Repair Facility. (See back pages for other specific entries.)

YEAR 20_____ DATE	RECORDING TACH TIME	TODAY'S FLIGHT	TOTAL TIME IN SERVICE	**Description of Inspections, Tests, Repairs and Alterations** Entries must be endorsed with Name, Rating and Certificate Number of Technician or Repair Facility. (See back pages for other specific entries.)

YEAR 20____ DATE	RECORDING TACH TIME	TODAY'S FLIGHT	TOTAL TIME IN SERVICE	**Description of Inspections, Tests, Repairs and Alterations** Entries must be endorsed with Name, Rating and Certificate Number of Technician or Repair Facility. (See back pages for other specific entries.)

YEAR 20____ DATE	RECORDING TACH TIME	TODAY'S FLIGHT	TOTAL TIME IN SERVICE	**Description of Inspections, Tests, Repairs and Alterations** Entries must be endorsed with Name, Rating and Certificate Number of Technician or Repair Facility. (See back pages for other specific entries.)

YEAR 20____ DATE	RECORDING TACH TIME	TODAY'S FLIGHT	TOTAL TIME IN SERVICE	**Description of Inspections, Tests, Repairs and Alterations** Entries must be endorsed with Name, Rating and Certificate Number of Technician or Repair Facility. (See back pages for other specific entries.)

YEAR 20____ DATE	RECORDING TACH TIME	TODAY'S FLIGHT	TOTAL TIME IN SERVICE	**Description of Inspections, Tests, Repairs and Alterations** Entries must be endorsed with Name, Rating and Certificate Number of Technician or Repair Facility. (See back pages for other specific entries.)

YEAR 20____ DATE	RECORDING TACH TIME	TODAY'S FLIGHT	TOTAL TIME IN SERVICE	**Description of Inspections, Tests, Repairs and Alterations** Entries must be endorsed with Name, Rating and Certificate Number of Technician or Repair Facility. (See back pages for other specific entries.)

YEAR 20____ DATE	RECORDING TACH TIME	TODAY'S FLIGHT	TOTAL TIME IN SERVICE	**Description of Inspections, Tests, Repairs and Alterations** Entries must be endorsed with Name, Rating and Certificate Number of Technician or Repair Facility. (See back pages for other specific entries.)

YEAR 20____ DATE	RECORDING TACH TIME	TODAY'S FLIGHT	TOTAL TIME IN SERVICE	**Description of Inspections, Tests, Repairs and Alterations** Entries must be endorsed with Name, Rating and Certificate Number of Technician or Repair Facility. (See back pages for other specific entries.)

YEAR 20____ DATE	RECORDING TACH TIME	TODAY'S FLIGHT	TOTAL TIME IN SERVICE	**Description of Inspections, Tests, Repairs and Alterations** Entries must be endorsed with Name, Rating and Certificate Number of Technician or Repair Facility. (See back pages for other specific entries.)

YEAR 20____ DATE	RECORDING TACH TIME	TODAY'S FLIGHT	TOTAL TIME IN SERVICE	**Description of Inspections, Tests, Repairs and Alterations** Entries must be endorsed with Name, Rating and Certificate Number of Technician or Repair Facility. (See back pages for other specific entries.)

YEAR 20____ DATE	RECORDING TACH TIME	TODAY'S FLIGHT	TOTAL TIME IN SERVICE	**Description of Inspections, Tests, Repairs and Alterations** Entries must be endorsed with Name, Rating and Certificate Number of Technician or Repair Facility. (See back pages for other specific entries.)

YEAR 20____ DATE	RECORDING TACH TIME	TODAY'S FLIGHT	TOTAL TIME IN SERVICE	**Description of Inspections, Tests, Repairs and Alterations** Entries must be endorsed with Name, Rating and Certificate Number of Technician or Repair Facility. (See back pages for other specific entries.)

YEAR 20_____ DATE	RECORDING TACH TIME	TODAY'S FLIGHT	TOTAL TIME IN SERVICE	**Description of Inspections, Tests, Repairs and Alterations** Entries must be endorsed with Name, Rating and Certificate Number of Technician or Repair Facility. (See back pages for other specific entries.)

YEAR 20_____ DATE	RECORDING TACH TIME	TODAY'S FLIGHT	TOTAL TIME IN SERVICE	**Description of Inspections, Tests, Repairs and Alterations** Entries must be endorsed with Name, Rating and Certificate Number of Technician or Repair Facility. (See back pages for other specific entries.)

YEAR 20_____ DATE	RECORDING TACH TIME	TODAY'S FLIGHT	TOTAL TIME IN SERVICE	**Description of Inspections, Tests, Repairs and Alterations** Entries must be endorsed with Name, Rating and Certificate Number of Technician or Repair Facility. (See back pages for other specific entries.)

YEAR 20____ DATE	RECORDING TACH TIME	TODAY'S FLIGHT	TOTAL TIME IN SERVICE	**Description of Inspections, Tests, Repairs and Alterations** Entries must be endorsed with Name, Rating and Certificate Number of Technician or Repair Facility. (See back pages for other specific entries.)

YEAR 20____ DATE	RECORDING TACH TIME	TODAY'S FLIGHT	TOTAL TIME IN SERVICE	**Description of Inspections, Tests, Repairs and Alterations** Entries must be endorsed with Name, Rating and Certificate Number of Technician or Repair Facility. (See back pages for other specific entries.)

YEAR 20_____ DATE	RECORDING TACH TIME	TODAY'S FLIGHT	TOTAL TIME IN SERVICE	**Description of Inspections, Tests, Repairs and Alterations** Entries must be endorsed with Name, Rating and Certificate Number of Technician or Repair Facility. (See back pages for other specific entries.)

YEAR 20_____ DATE	RECORDING TACH TIME	TODAY'S FLIGHT	TOTAL TIME IN SERVICE	**Description of Inspections, Tests, Repairs and Alterations** Entries must be endorsed with Name, Rating and Certificate Number of Technician or Repair Facility. (See back pages for other specific entries.)

YEAR 20____ DATE	RECORDING TACH TIME	TODAY'S FLIGHT	TOTAL TIME IN SERVICE	**Description of Inspections, Tests, Repairs and Alterations** Entries must be endorsed with Name, Rating and Certificate Number of Technician or Repair Facility. (See back pages for other specific entries.)

YEAR 20_____ DATE	RECORDING TACH TIME	TODAY'S FLIGHT	TOTAL TIME IN SERVICE	**Description of Inspections, Tests, Repairs and Alterations** Entries must be endorsed with Name, Rating and Certificate Number of Technician or Repair Facility. (See back pages for other specific entries.)

YEAR **20____** **DATE**	**RECORDING TACH TIME**	**TODAY'S FLIGHT**	**TOTAL TIME IN SERVICE**	**Description of Inspections, Tests, Repairs and Alterations** Entries must be endorsed with Name, Rating and Certificate Number of Technician or Repair Facility. (See back pages for other specific entries.)

YEAR 20____ DATE	RECORDING TACH TIME	TODAY'S FLIGHT	TOTAL TIME IN SERVICE	**Description of Inspections, Tests, Repairs and Alterations** Entries must be endorsed with Name, Rating and Certificate Number of Technician or Repair Facility. (See back pages for other specific entries.)

YEAR 20____ DATE	RECORDING TACH TIME	TODAY'S FLIGHT	TOTAL TIME IN SERVICE	**Description of Inspections, Tests, Repairs and Alterations** Entries must be endorsed with Name, Rating and Certificate Number of Technician or Repair Facility. (See back pages for other specific entries.)

YEAR 20_____ DATE	RECORDING TACH TIME	TODAY'S FLIGHT	TOTAL TIME IN SERVICE	**Description of Inspections, Tests, Repairs and Alterations** Entries must be endorsed with Name, Rating and Certificate Number of Technician or Repair Facility. (See back pages for other specific entries.)

YEAR 20____ DATE	RECORDING TACH TIME	TODAY'S FLIGHT	TOTAL TIME IN SERVICE	**Description of Inspections, Tests, Repairs and Alterations** Entries must be endorsed with Name, Rating and Certificate Number of Technician or Repair Facility. (See back pages for other specific entries.)

YEAR 20____ DATE	RECORDING TACH TIME	TODAY'S FLIGHT	TOTAL TIME IN SERVICE	**Description of Inspections, Tests, Repairs and Alterations** Entries must be endorsed with Name, Rating and Certificate Number of Technician or Repair Facility. (See back pages for other specific entries.)

YEAR 20____ DATE	RECORDING TACH TIME	TODAY'S FLIGHT	TOTAL TIME IN SERVICE	**Description of Inspections, Tests, Repairs and Alterations** Entries must be endorsed with Name, Rating and Certificate Number of Technician or Repair Facility. (See back pages for other specific entries.)

YEAR 20_____ DATE	RECORDING TACH TIME	TODAY'S FLIGHT	TOTAL TIME IN SERVICE	**Description of Inspections, Tests, Repairs and Alterations** Entries must be endorsed with Name, Rating and Certificate Number of Technician or Repair Facility. (See back pages for other specific entries.)

YEAR 20____ DATE	RECORDING TACH TIME	TODAY'S FLIGHT	TOTAL TIME IN SERVICE	**Description of Inspections, Tests, Repairs and Alterations** Entries must be endorsed with Name, Rating and Certificate Number of Technician or Repair Facility. (See back pages for other specific entries.)

YEAR 20_____ **DATE**	**RECORDING TACH TIME**	**TODAY'S FLIGHT**	**TOTAL TIME IN SERVICE**	**Description of Inspections, Tests, Repairs and Alterations** Entries must be endorsed with Name, Rating and Certificate Number of Technician or Repair Facility. (See back pages for other specific entries.)

YEAR 20_____ DATE	RECORDING TACH TIME	TODAY'S FLIGHT	TOTAL TIME IN SERVICE	**Description of Inspections, Tests, Repairs and Alterations** Entries must be endorsed with Name, Rating and Certificate Number of Technician or Repair Facility. (See back pages for other specific entries.)

YEAR 20_____ DATE	RECORDING TACH TIME	TODAY'S FLIGHT	TOTAL TIME IN SERVICE	**Description of Inspections, Tests, Repairs and Alterations** Entries must be endorsed with Name, Rating and Certificate Number of Technician or Repair Facility. (See back pages for other specific entries.)

YEAR 20______ DATE	RECORDING TACH TIME	TODAY'S FLIGHT	TOTAL TIME IN SERVICE	**Description of Inspections, Tests, Repairs and Alterations** Entries must be endorsed with Name, Rating and Certificate Number of Technician or Repair Facility. (See back pages for other specific entries.)

YEAR 20_____ DATE	RECORDING TACH TIME	TODAY'S FLIGHT	TOTAL TIME IN SERVICE	**Description of Inspections, Tests, Repairs and Alterations** Entries must be endorsed with Name, Rating and Certificate Number of Technician or Repair Facility. (See back pages for other specific entries.)

YEAR 20_____ DATE	RECORDING TACH TIME	TODAY'S FLIGHT	TOTAL TIME IN SERVICE	**Description of Inspections, Tests, Repairs and Alterations** Entries must be endorsed with Name, Rating and Certificate Number of Technician or Repair Facility. (See back pages for other specific entries.)

YEAR 20____ DATE	RECORDING TACH TIME	TODAY'S FLIGHT	TOTAL TIME IN SERVICE	**Description of Inspections, Tests, Repairs and Alterations** Entries must be endorsed with Name, Rating and Certificate Number of Technician or Repair Facility. (See back pages for other specific entries.)

YEAR 20_____ DATE	RECORDING TACH TIME	TODAY'S FLIGHT	TOTAL TIME IN SERVICE	**Description of Inspections, Tests, Repairs and Alterations** Entries must be endorsed with Name, Rating and Certificate Number of Technician or Repair Facility. (See back pages for other specific entries.)

YEAR 20____ DATE	RECORDING TACH TIME	TODAY'S FLIGHT	TOTAL TIME IN SERVICE	**Description of Inspections, Tests, Repairs and Alterations** Entries must be endorsed with Name, Rating and Certificate Number of Technician or Repair Facility. (See back pages for other specific entries.)

YEAR 20____ DATE	RECORDING TACH TIME	TODAY'S FLIGHT	TOTAL TIME IN SERVICE	**Description of Inspections, Tests, Repairs and Alterations** Entries must be endorsed with Name, Rating and Certificate Number of Technician or Repair Facility. (See back pages for other specific entries.)

YEAR 20____ DATE	RECORDING TACH TIME	TODAY'S FLIGHT	TOTAL TIME IN SERVICE	**Description of Inspections, Tests, Repairs and Alterations** Entries must be endorsed with Name, Rating and Certificate Number of Technician or Repair Facility. (See back pages for other specific entries.)

YEAR 20_____ DATE	RECORDING TACH TIME	TODAY'S FLIGHT	TOTAL TIME IN SERVICE	**Description of Inspections, Tests, Repairs and Alterations** Entries must be endorsed with Name, Rating and Certificate Number of Technician or Repair Facility. (See back pages for other specific entries.)

YEAR 20____ DATE	RECORDING TACH TIME	TODAY'S FLIGHT	TOTAL TIME IN SERVICE	**Description of Inspections, Tests, Repairs and Alterations** Entries must be endorsed with Name, Rating and Certificate Number of Technician or Repair Facility. (See back pages for other specific entries.)

YEAR 20_____ DATE	RECORDING TACH TIME	TODAY'S FLIGHT	TOTAL TIME IN SERVICE	**Description of Inspections, Tests, Repairs and Alterations** Entries must be endorsed with Name, Rating and Certificate Number of Technician or Repair Facility. (See back pages for other specific entries.)

YEAR 20____ DATE	RECORDING TACH TIME	TODAY'S FLIGHT	TOTAL TIME IN SERVICE	**Description of Inspections, Tests, Repairs and Alterations** Entries must be endorsed with Name, Rating and Certificate Number of Technician or Repair Facility. (See back pages for other specific entries.)

YEAR 20____ DATE	RECORDING TACH TIME	TODAY'S FLIGHT	TOTAL TIME IN SERVICE	**Description of Inspections, Tests, Repairs and Alterations** Entries must be endorsed with Name, Rating and Certificate Number of Technician or Repair Facility. (See back pages for other specific entries.)

YEAR 20____ DATE	TOTAL TIME IN SERVICE	**Reference of Major Repairs and Major Alterations To** FAA Form 337 by Date, or to the Work Order by Number and the Approving Agency

YEAR 20_____ DATE	TOTAL TIME IN SERVICE	**Reference of Major Repairs and Major Alterations To** FAA Form 337 by Date, or to the Work Order by Number and the Approving Agency

YEAR 20_____ DATE	TOTAL TIME IN SERVICE	**Reference of Major Repairs and Major Alterations To** FAA Form 337 by Date, or to the Work Order by Number and the Approving Agency

YEAR 20_____ DATE	A.D. NUMBER	TOTAL TIME IN SERVICE	**Airworthiness Directives** Chronological Listing of Compliance and Method of Compliance

YEAR 20____ DATE	A.D. NUMBER	TOTAL TIME IN SERVICE	**Airworthiness Directives** Chronological Listing of Compliance and Method of Compliance

YEAR 20____ DATE	A.D. NUMBER	TOTAL TIME IN SERVICE	**Airworthiness Directives** Chronological Listing of Compliance and Method of Compliance

YEAR 20____ DATE	TOTAL TIME IN SERVICE	**Manufacturer's Mandatory Service Bulletins** Chronological Listing of Compliance and Method of Compliance

YEAR 20____ DATE	TOTAL TIME IN SERVICE	**Equipment Addition, Removal or Exchange** Item Manufacturer's Name Model Serial Number	
			☐ Addition of Optional Equipment ☐ Removal of Optional Equipment ☐ Addition of Required—Exchanged for Optional ☐ Removal of Required—Exchanged for Optional
			☐ Addition of Optional Equipment ☐ Removal of Optional Equipment ☐ Addition of Required—Exchanged for Optional ☐ Removal of Required—Exchanged for Optional
			☐ Addition of Optional Equipment ☐ Removal of Optional Equipment ☐ Addition of Required—Exchanged for Optional ☐ Removal of Required—Exchanged for Optional
			☐ Addition of Optional Equipment ☐ Removal of Optional Equipment ☐ Addition of Required—Exchanged for Optional ☐ Removal of Required—Exchanged for Optional
			☐ Addition of Optional Equipment ☐ Removal of Optional Equipment ☐ Addition of Required—Exchanged for Optional ☐ Removal of Required—Exchanged for Optional
			☐ Addition of Optional Equipment ☐ Removal of Optional Equipment ☐ Addition of Required—Exchanged for Optional ☐ Removal of Required—Exchanged for Optional

YEAR 20_____ DATE	TOTAL TIME IN SERVICE	**Equipment Addition, Removal or Exchange** Item / Manufacturer's Name / Model / Serial Number	
			☐ Addition of Optional Equipment ☐ Removal of Optional Equipment ☐ Addition of Required—Exchanged for Optional ☐ Removal of Required—Exchanged for Optional
			☐ Addition of Optional Equipment ☐ Removal of Optional Equipment ☐ Addition of Required—Exchanged for Optional ☐ Removal of Required—Exchanged for Optional
			☐ Addition of Optional Equipment ☐ Removal of Optional Equipment ☐ Addition of Required—Exchanged for Optional ☐ Removal of Required—Exchanged for Optional
			☐ Addition of Optional Equipment ☐ Removal of Optional Equipment ☐ Addition of Required—Exchanged for Optional ☐ Removal of Required—Exchanged for Optional
			☐ Addition of Optional Equipment ☐ Removal of Optional Equipment ☐ Addition of Required—Exchanged for Optional ☐ Removal of Required—Exchanged for Optional
			☐ Addition of Optional Equipment ☐ Removal of Optional Equipment ☐ Addition of Required—Exchanged for Optional ☐ Removal of Required—Exchanged for Optional

Notes

Notes